The NatureTrail Book of PONDS & STREAMS

Su Swallow

Identifying Freshwater Animals and Plants with this Book

This book is about common birds, mammals, plants, fishes, insects, frogs and other creatures that you will find in or near fresh water. When you find or see something, and you want to know what it is, use this book as follows:

Turn to the pages which deal with the **kind of animal or plant** you have seen. For example, pages 24–25 tell you about frogs. If you can't see a picture of it there . . .

. . . turn to the back of the book (pages 28–31) and look it up in the section called **More Freshwater Life to Spot,** where you may be able to find a picture of it.

Always make careful notes about the things that you see, and try to identify them later.

First published in 1977 by
Usborne Publishing Ltd,
20 Garrick Street,
London WC2

Written by
Su Swallow

Edited by
Ingrid Selberg

Consultant Editor
Alfred Leutscher, B.Sc., F.Z.S.

Special advice from
Peter Holden, Chris Humphries,
Alwyne Wheeler, Anthony Wootton

Designed by
Sally Burrough

Illustrated by
John Barber, Joyce Bee, Hilary
Burn, Don Forrest, Christine
Howes, Annabel Milne and Peter
Stebbing, Richard Orr, Phil Weare,
John Yates

Printed in Belgium

The NatureTrail Book of
PONDS & STREAMS

About This Book

This book tells you where to
look for common birds, fishes,
insects, mammals, plants and
amphibians in and around
fresh water in Europe.
It shows you clues to look for,
how water animals and plants
live and how to collect and
keep live specimens
for study at home.

Contents

How to Start

The best time to study streams and ponds is in the spring and summer, when the plants are flowering and the animals are most active. But winter is a very good time to spot birds.

Move slowly and quietly and be careful your shadow does not alarm the fishes. You will find more life near the bank, where there is more plant cover.

Look for freshwater life in lakes, rivers, ditches and canals. You may even find plants or insects in drinking troughs and rainwater tubs.

What to Take

Empty margarine pot for watching animals

Fishing net

Jars

Binoculars

Magnifying glass

A Pond Survey

Ask some friends to help make a map of your pond, showing the plants and animals you find. If you look carefully, you might find something rare. Repeat the survey to see how pond life changes with the seasons. Check for signs of pollution. You can survey part of a stream in exactly the same way.

What to Look for

Even a small pond can support a surprising variety of life if it is not too shaded or polluted. Here are some of the animals to look for and their hiding places.

REMEMBER! NEVER GO INTO THE WATER IF YOU CAN'T SWIM. IT IS BEST TO GO WITH A FRIEND. DON'T WADE INTO RIVERS OR DEEP STREAMS. THERE MAY BE STRONG CURRENTS.

DO'S AND DON'TS

DO TEST WATER DEPTH WITH A LONG POLE BEFORE WADING IN.

DON'T USE LOGS OR STONES AS STEPPING-STONES WITHOUT TESTING THEM FIRST.

DO REPLACE STONES AND LOGS EXACTLY AS YOU FOUND THEM.

DO KEEP JARS WITH SPECIMENS IN THE SHADE TO KEEP THE WATER COOL.

DON'T HANDLE ANYTHING YOU CATCH. PUT IT STRAIGHT INTO A DISH OR JAR.

DON'T SMASH ICE ON PONDS IN WINTER. THIS WILL DISTURB ANIMALS LIVING THERE.

DON'T STAMP YOUR FEET OR MOVE QUICKLY. THIS WILL FRIGHTEN ANIMALS.

DON'T TAKE TOO MANY ANIMALS OR WHOLE PLANTS. PART OF A PLANT WILL BE ENOUGH TO IDENTIFY IT.

DO PUT ANIMALS AND PLANTS BACK INTO THE POND AS SOON AS POSSIBLE.

Damselfly

Frogspawn

Look underneath water plants for eggs and small animals.

Great Diving Beetle

Look under stones for worms, insects and leeches.

Stonefly nymph

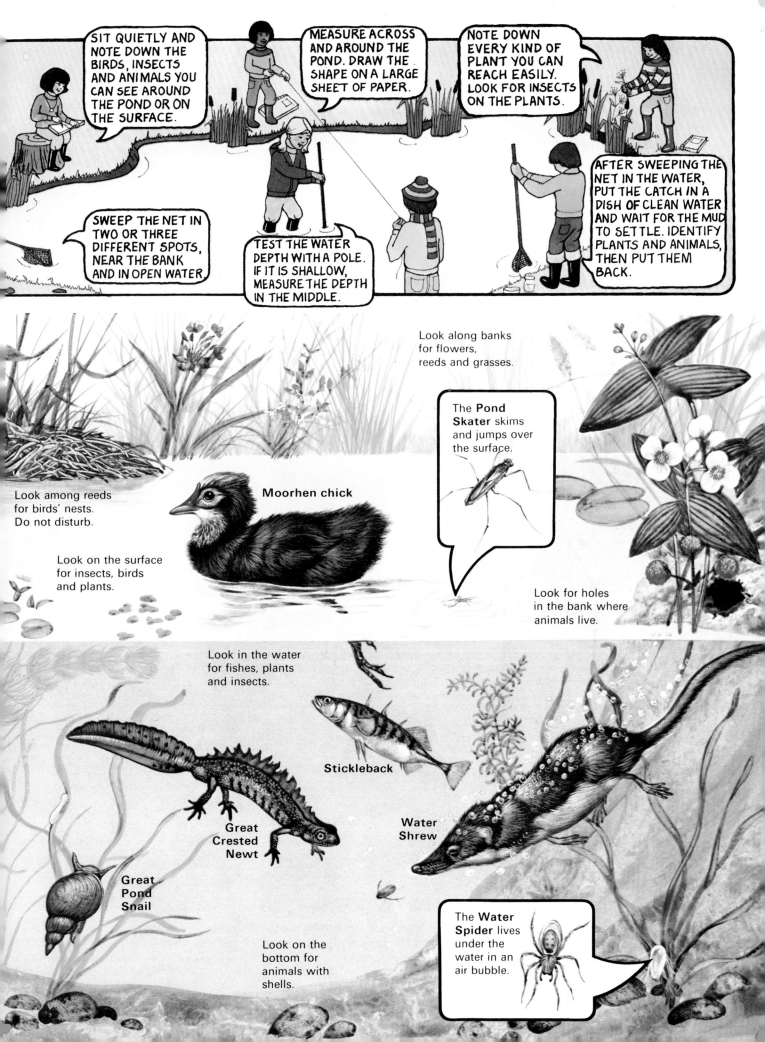

Living Together

In a thriving pond there is a balance of different kinds of animals and plants, so that there is enough food for them all to survive. It is important not to disturb this balance.

How Plants Help

Animals living in water need a gas called oxygen to breathe. They get some from the surface, but water plants also give off oxygen when they make their food. Plants need sunlight to make food and produce oxygen.

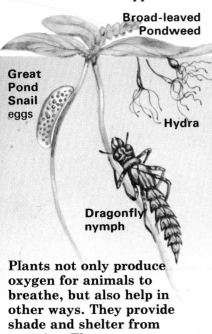

Canadian Pondweed

Try this experiment: put some Canadian Pondweed in water in the sun. Oxygen bubbles will soon appear.

Broad-leaved Pondweed

Great Pond Snail eggs

Hydra

Dragonfly nymph

Plants not only produce oxygen for animals to breathe, but also help in other ways. They provide shade and shelter from enemies. They act as supports for eggs and tiny animals. Some insects use plant stems to climb out of the water when they are changing into winged adults.

Pond Food Chain

The process of one animal eating another and then being eaten by a larger animal is called a food chain. In the chain shown here, there are six links joined by arrows. At the top is the Heron which eats everything in the second link including Perch. Perch eat animals in the third link and so on down to the Algae at the bottom. Because each animal eats many things, a pond has many different food chains.

There are more animals at the bottom of the chain than at the top. This is because these animals are small, and a larger animal needs to eat many of them to survive.

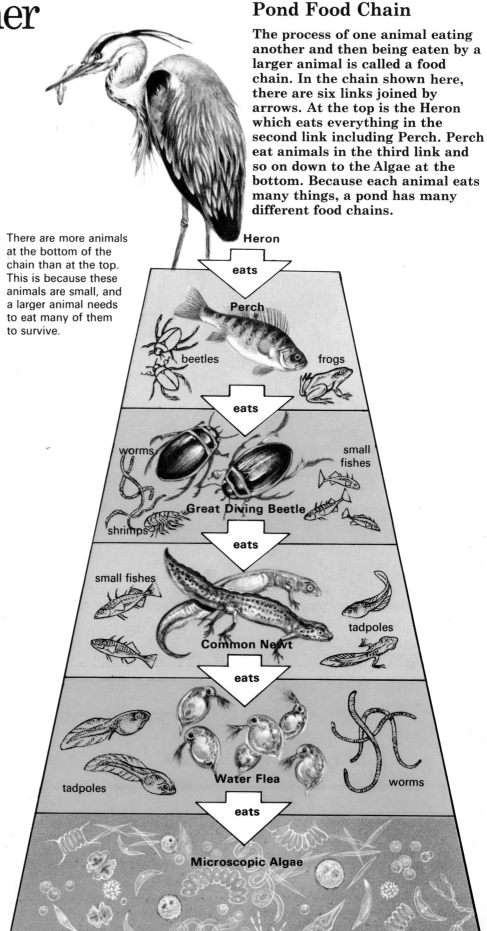

Heron

eats

Perch

beetles

frogs

eats

worms

small fishes

Great Diving Beetle

shrimps

eats

small fishes

tadpoles

Common Newt

eats

tadpoles

Water Flea

worms

eats

Microscopic Algae

Pollution

Here are some of the ways that fresh water can become so polluted that the plants and animals in it die.

Insecticides, sprayed on crops, are spread by the wind and rain into the river where they poison fishes.

The stream is clear and unpolluted at its source.

Overhanging trees block out light from pond plants. Fallen leaves use up oxygen as they rot.

Rain washes agricultural fertilizers into the water, which makes water plants grow faster and use too much oxygen.

Rubbish dumped into ponds poisons the water and kills pond life. Too many ducks can eat up all the plants in the pond.

Mining wastes float on the water surface and block out light from the plants below. Some pieces settle into spaces in the river bed where animals live.

Water sports can disturb animal and plant life.

Warm water, which is produced by cooling processes in factories, is emptied into the river. This kills fishes that need cool water.

Poisons from papermills and chemical factories kill fishes and make the water smell bad.

Sewage waste, which is emptied into water, uses up oxygen, so that animals die. Fungus grows and kills off plants.

Ponds . . .   . . . and Streams

Thick vegetation

Little vegetation

Carp

Trout

Mud bottom

Stony bottom

The kinds of animals and plants you find depend on whether the water is flowing or still. The water's temperature, how much oxygen it contains and the type of bottom are also important.

Plants root easily in the still water of a pond. The lush vegetation encourages many animals to live there. Ponds may freeze in winter, killing many animals.

Few plants can grow in fast-flowing streams. Look for Algae and small animals that cling to the bottom. Some fishes only thrive in running water. Where the water moves slowly, it is more like a pond.

Plants of Ponds and Streams

Pond plants can be divided into groups depending on the zones, or areas, where they grow. Remember that the zones often overlap, and that you may not find all of the zones in one pond. Many of these common freshwater plants also grow in streams and rivers.

Notice how delicate many of the plants in deep water are. They do not need thick stems to support them, because the water holds them up. Their leaves are rather fine and thin because they do not need to hold water as land plants do.

Swallow

The **Common Reed** is Britain's tallest grass and grows up to 3 m tall. It often grows on river banks where its roots hold the soil firm.

Only the flower spikes of the **Spiked Water Milfoil** grow above the water.

Frogbit flowers in July and August.

The **Water Crowfoot** and **Broad-leaved Pondweed** have two kinds of leaves: large, flat leaves floating on the water, and fine leaves under the water.

Duckweed may cover a whole pond. It hardly ever flowers.

Canadian Pondweed spreads so quickly that it sometimes chokes other water plants.

Broad-leaved Pondweed

Water Crowfoot

Tadpole

Algae are microscopic plants that look like green slime.

Stickleback

Deep Water Zone

Underwater Plants

In the middle of the pond, plants grow under the water, apart from some of the flower heads which rise above the surface. Their roots are in the mud.

Floating Plants

Some plants that grow near the centre of the pond float with their roots hanging free in the water.

Rooted Plants

Plants growing in fairly shallow water around the edge of this zone have their roots in the mud. Their leaves either float or stand out of the water.

The dark brown top of
the **Great Reedmace**
is made up of seeds.

Meadowsweet
has clusters of
sweet-smelling,
feathery flowers on
tall stems.

The flowers of the
Water Plantain
only open in the
afternoon.

**Great
Pond
Sedge**

Soft Rush

Look on shady
banks for the
**Water Forget-
me-not**.

The large leaves
and strong roots
of the **Marsh
Marigold** are
typical of
bankside plants.

Shallow Water Zone

Plants found in the shallow water
zone are usually tall with long
underground stems, called
rhizomes, to hold them upright.
These rhizomes spread and may
crowd out the other plants.

Bankside Zone

The banks of ponds and streams
have soft, damp soil. Many
different kinds of plants can grow
there, and they are often brightly
coloured. Notice how many of
the plants have large leaves, and
strong roots to hold them firmly in
the soil.

Stream and River Plants

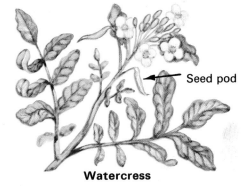

Seed pod

Watercress

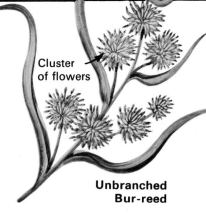

Cluster
of flowers

**Unbranched
Bur-reed**

Tiny green
flowers in
June and
July

Marestail

Watercress grows in fast-
flowing streams. Look out for
its long seed pods. Do not eat
wild Watercress.

Look in shallow, slow-moving
water for this plant. You may
find other kinds of Bur-reed
in ponds.

Marestail sometimes grows
completely under the water. Its
tiny flowers are very simple and
have no petals.

How Water Plants Grow

Many water plants grow from seeds. The seeds are formed after pollen from the male part of the flower (the stamen) reaches the female part (the style) of the same kind of flower. When the seeds are ripe, they are scattered and some of them grow. Some water plants can also spread by growing new plants from their rhizomes, or underground stems.

Some underwater plants do not spread by seed. Instead, new plants may grow from winter buds or from pieces that break off the old plant.

1 How Pollen Spreads

Purple Loosestrife

Water Mint

Pollen from some plants is spread by insects. The bright colours and scent attract insects, and the pollen rubs off on to their bodies. Then they carry it to other plants.

2

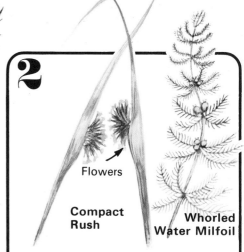

Flowers

Compact Rush

Whorled Water Milfoil

Plants like these are pollinated by the wind. Their flowers are often small and dull, because they do not need to attract insects.

How Seeds are Scattered

By Wind

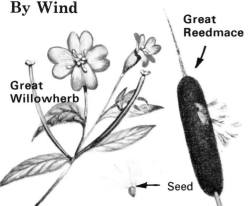

Great Reedmace

Great Willowherb

Seed

Some seeds are carried by the wind on a hairy parachute. Willowherb seeds may travel as far away as 150 kilometres.

By Water

Yellow Iris

Seed pods

Some plant seeds, like these pods from a Yellow Iris, are carried by water. They open when softened by water.

By Animals

Bristle with barbs

Seed

Bur Marigold

Seeds with barbs, or hooks, catch on to animals' fur or people's clothing and later drop off.

How Water Lilies Grow

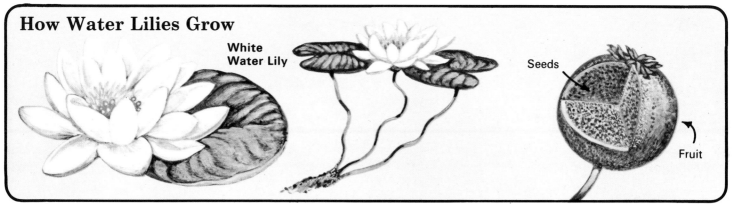

White Water Lily

Seeds

Fruit

Look in ponds for the White Water Lily. Its leaves and flowers float on the surface, but at night the flowers close, and sometimes sink just below the surface until morning.

The Water Lily is anchored to the bottom by stout rhizomes. The leaf stalks grow up from these stems at an angle. If the water level rises, they straighten up so that the leaves can still float.

The flowers are pollinated by insects. When the fruits are ripe, they sink to the bottom and release up to 2,000 seeds. The seeds float away, and some sink and start to grow into new plants.

3

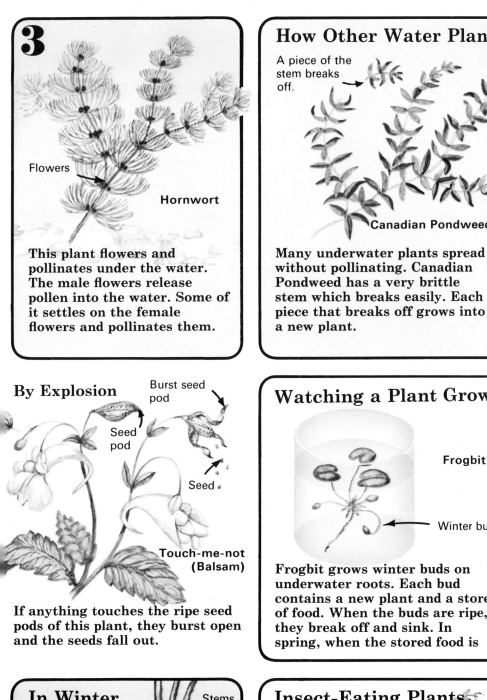

Flowers

Hornwort

This plant flowers and pollinates under the water. The male flowers release pollen into the water. Some of it settles on the female flowers and pollinates them.

How Other Water Plants Spread

A piece of the stem breaks off.

Two new leaves grow out of an old one.

Canadian Pondweed

Ivy Duckweed

Many underwater plants spread without pollinating. Canadian Pondweed has a very brittle stem which breaks easily. Each piece that breaks off grows into a new plant.

Ivy Duckweed grows under the water, just below the surface. Each tiny leaf is a separate plant. New leaves grow out of slits in the sides of old ones and then break away to become new plants.

By Explosion

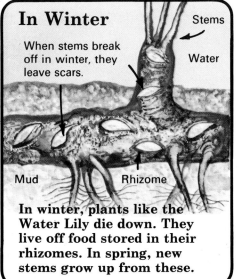

Burst seed pod

Seed pod

Seed

Touch-me-not (Balsam)

If anything touches the ripe seed pods of this plant, they burst open and the seeds fall out.

Watching a Plant Grow

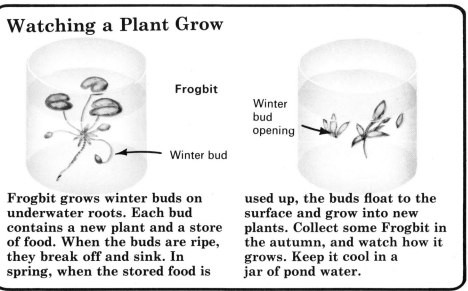

Frogbit

Winter bud

Winter bud opening

Frogbit grows winter buds on underwater roots. Each bud contains a new plant and a store of food. When the buds are ripe, they break off and sink. In spring, when the stored food is

used up, the buds float to the surface and grow into new plants. Collect some Frogbit in the autumn, and watch how it grows. Keep it cool in a jar of pond water.

In Winter

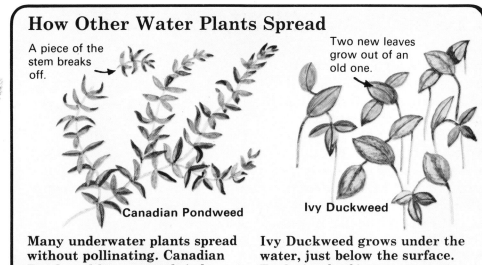

Stems

When stems break off in winter, they leave scars.

Water

Mud

Rhizome

In winter, plants like the Water Lily die down. They live off food stored in their rhizomes. In spring, new stems grow up from these.

Insect-Eating Plants

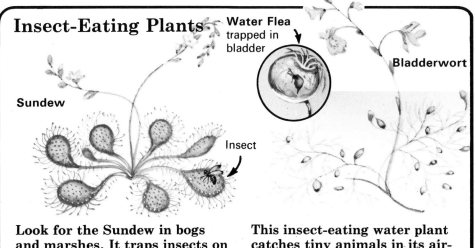

Water Flea trapped in bladder

Bladderwort

Sundew

Insect

Look for the Sundew in bogs and marshes. It traps insects on its hairs and digests them with special juices.

This insect-eating water plant catches tiny animals in its air-filled, underwater bladders. Then it feeds on them.

Watching Water Birds

Birdwatching by ponds and streams is exciting because of the variety of birds you may find there. Some birds spend most of their lives by water. Others may come to drink and bathe. In winter, sea birds fly inland for food and shelter.

The best place to look for birds is by water surrounded by thick vegetation. Early morning is a good time to see them.

In parks, some water birds are tame enough to be fed. Others are shy, so you must hide and wait quietly to see them. Keep a record of the birds you spot and their habits. If you find a nest, be sure not to disturb it.

Feeding

Watch the birds on and around a pond closely. See how many ways of feeding you can spot, the different bill shapes and how they are suited to these feeding methods. Time how long diving ducks stay under the water.

Mallards are dabbling ducks. They feed near the surface and eat mostly plants. They also up-end to get food from deep water.

Tufted Ducks dive down one or two metres for water plants, insects and small fishes.

Female   Male

Wigeon feed mainly on grasses and grain, cropped from fields. They also dabble in water.

The **Swift** feeds and even sleeps on the wing. It eats flies and beetles.

The **Shoveler** uses its wide bill to sieve food from water and mud.

The **Teal** is Britain's smallest duck. It is a surface-feeder and eats mainly water plants and their seeds.

The **Bittern** nests in reed beds where it is camouflaged well. It eats frogs, small fishes and insects.

The **Moorhen** eats plants and small animals in the water as well as seeds and grain on land.

The **Kingfisher** dives for small fishes and insects. It sometimes beats a fish against a branch to kill it. Then it swallows the fish head first, so that the fins and scales do not open and choke the bird.

Flocks in Flight

1 Taking a Count

To work out the number of birds in a flock, count the first ten birds. Then guess what part that is of the whole flock. Multiply to get the total number of birds.

2 Flight Patterns

Geese in V-shape

Ducks in straight line

The pattern a flock forms can help you to identify the birds. Many birds fly in a line or a V-shape.

3 Keeping Together

Common Sandpiper

Redshank

Birds that fly in flocks usually have distinctive markings for others to follow. They also call to each other to keep together, especially after dark.

The **Greylag Goose** spends a lot of time on land. It crops the grass with its bill.

Looking after Feathers

1 Bathing

Goosander

Water birds often bathe to keep clean. They flap their wings on the water and roll over to wet their bodies thoroughly. Then they shake themselves dry.

2 Oiling

Great Crested Grebe

Preen gland

Next, water birds spread oil from the preen glands near their tails, by rubbing their bills and heads over their feathers. The oil is good for the condition of the feathers.

3 Preening

Pintail

Finally, they fluff up their feathers, nibble each one and draw them through their bills. This cleans and oils them still more, and settles them back into place.

How Feathers Work

Duck feather

Shaft

Barb

The barbs on a bird's feather grow out of the shaft. They fit together very closely, rather like the teeth of a zip. This helps keep the bird's body dry and warm.

Birds: Mating and Nesting

Birds become very active in the spring when most of them breed. The male birds attract females by showing off their bright feathers. Some develop crests and ruffs of feathers at this time. They make special mating calls and perform acrobatics in the air or on the water. Sometimes both male and female birds take part in these courtship displays.

When the female has accepted the male, a nest is built. Notice what materials each kind of bird collects for its nest.

Courtship

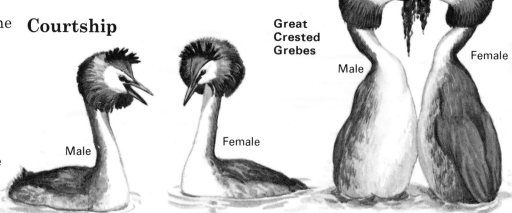

Great Crested Grebes

Male

Female

Male

Female

Great Crested Grebes start their courtship early in the year. Head-shaking (above) is a common display. The birds swim towards each other, calling and shaking their heads from side to side.

After head-shaking, the Grebes may "dance" together. First they dive to collect weed. Then they swim towards one another and rise out of the water, swaying their bills and paddling hard.

Fighting

Mute Swan

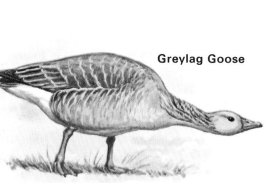

Greylag Goose

Coots

This Swan is puffing out its feathers to frighten away an enemy. Sometimes birds fight to defend their nest or territory.

This Greylag Goose is standing in a threat position to chase away other adult geese that might come too close to its nest or territory.

Coots fight with their claws, holding themselves up with their wings. Fights do not last very long, and usually only the males take part.

Nesting

Reed Warblers

Sand Martins

Dippers

The Reed Warbler nests in reed beds. The grass nest is shaped like a deep basket, so that the eggs and young birds cannot fall out, even in a strong wind.

Look for groups of Sand Martins nesting in mud or sand banks. Each nest is at the end of a tunnel, which the birds dig with their feet and bills.

The Dipper hides its nest in cracks between rocks near a stream. It also nests under bridges or behind waterfalls. The cup-shaped nest is made of moss and grasses.

Kingfishers

Female

Male

Male

Mallards

Female

Female

Male

Pochards

Some male birds, like the Kingfisher, make a present of food to the female during courtship. When she has accepted it, they are ready to mate.

The Mallard is a common duck, and you are quite likely to see the male's striking courtship display. He dives, flaps his wings, sprays water with his bill, whistles and grunts. The female draws his

attention by jerking her head to and fro.

To impress a female, the male Pochard swims around her, jerking his head backwards and forwards.

Looking after the Young

Grey Herons

Some birds, like the Heron, are born helpless. They are blind, featherless, and cannot leave the nest for over a month. Young Herons beg for food by pecking at their parents' bills. Other young

birds beg with loud cries or gaping beaks. However, some chicks, like Ducks and Grebes, can swim a few hours after hatching. Ducklings can also feed themselves.

Keeping the Young Safe

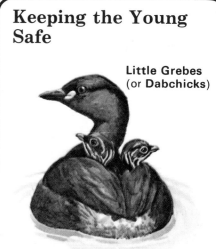

Little Grebes
(or Dabchicks)

Little Grebes can swim soon after they hatch, but sometimes they climb on to their parents' backs to keep safe from danger.

Little Ringed Plover

Like many other birds that nest on the ground, the Little Ringed Plover may pretend to be hurt to draw an enemy away from its nest.

How Insects Grow

You can find some strange and exciting insects in ponds and streams, even in polluted water. Most insects go through several stages of development between the egg and the adult. (Follow the steps in the development of the Caddis Fly.) The early stages may last for years, but the adult may live only for a few hours or days.

Some water insects, like water beetles, spend all their lives in the water, while others, like the Alder Fly, leave the water when fully grown.

The Caddis Fly

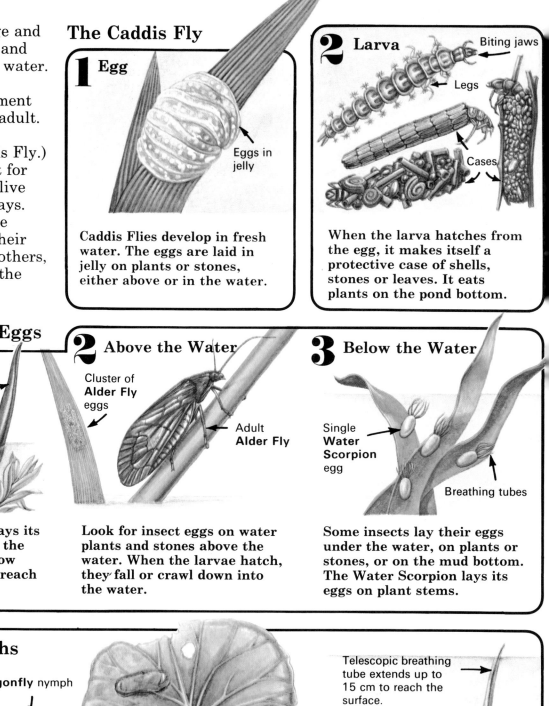

1 Egg

Eggs in jelly

Caddis Flies develop in fresh water. The eggs are laid in jelly on plants or stones, either above or in the water.

2 Larva

Biting jaws

Legs

Cases

When the larva hatches from the egg, it makes itself a protective case of shells, stones or leaves. It eats plants on the pond bottom.

Where Insects Lay Eggs

1 On the Water

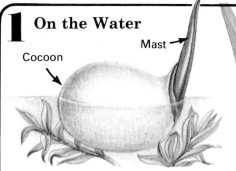

Mast

Cocoon

The Great Silver Beetle lays its eggs in a silky cocoon on the water's surface. The hollow "mast" is to allow air to reach the eggs.

2 Above the Water

Cluster of **Alder Fly** eggs

Adult **Alder Fly**

Look for insect eggs on water plants and stones above the water. When the larvae hatch, they fall or crawl down into the water.

3 Below the Water

Single **Water Scorpion** egg

Breathing tubes

Some insects lay their eggs under the water, on plants or stones, or on the mud bottom. The Water Scorpion lays its eggs on plant stems.

Larvae and Nymphs

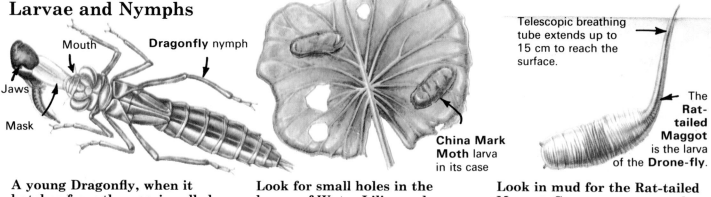

Mouth

Dragonfly nymph

Jaws

Mask

China Mark
Moth larva
in its case

Telescopic breathing tube extends up to 15 cm to reach the surface.

The
**Rat-tailed
Maggot**
is the larva
of the **Drone-fly**.

A young Dragonfly, when it hatches from the egg, is called a nymph. It has a strong pair of jaws fixed to a hinge, called a mask. The mask shoots out to catch prey.

Look for small holes in the leaves of Water Lilies and Pondweed. Underneath, you may see this moth larva, which makes a case out of the leaves and also feeds on them.

Look in mud for the Rat-tailed Maggot. Scoop up some mud and a little water in a dish, and wait for it to settle. Look for the Maggot's breathing tube.

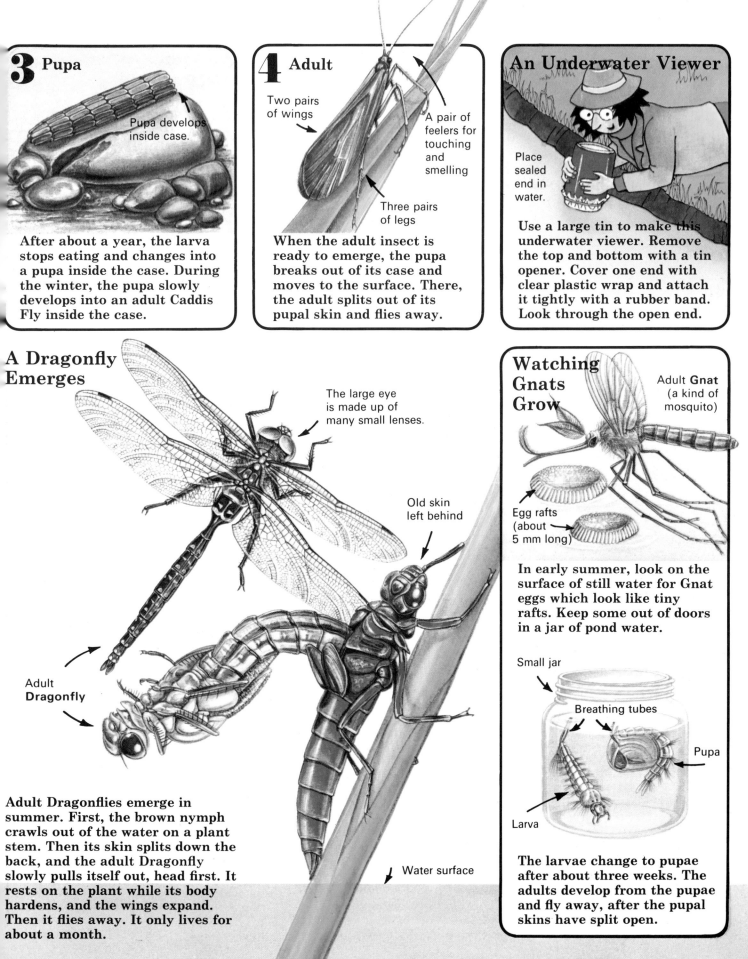

3 Pupa

Pupa develops inside case.

After about a year, the larva stops eating and changes into a pupa inside the case. During the winter, the pupa slowly develops into an adult Caddis Fly inside the case.

4 Adult

Two pairs of wings

A pair of feelers for touching and smelling

Three pairs of legs

When the adult insect is ready to emerge, the pupa breaks out of its case and moves to the surface. There, the adult splits out of its pupal skin and flies away.

An Underwater Viewer

Place sealed end in water.

Use a large tin to make this underwater viewer. Remove the top and bottom with a tin opener. Cover one end with clear plastic wrap and attach it tightly with a rubber band. Look through the open end.

A Dragonfly Emerges

The large eye is made up of many small lenses.

Old skin left behind

Adult **Dragonfly**

Adult Dragonflies emerge in summer. First, the brown nymph crawls out of the water on a plant stem. Then its skin splits down the back, and the adult Dragonfly slowly pulls itself out, head first. It rests on the plant while its body hardens, and the wings expand. Then it flies away. It only lives for about a month.

Water surface

Watching Gnats Grow

Adult **Gnat** (a kind of mosquito)

Egg rafts (about 5 mm long)

In early summer, look on the surface of still water for Gnat eggs which look like tiny rafts. Keep some out of doors in a jar of pond water.

Small jar

Breathing tubes

Pupa

Larva

The larvae change to pupae after about three weeks. The adults develop from the pupae and fly away, after the pupal skins have split open.

Watching Insects

If you sit by a pond or stream, you will soon spot several kinds of insects. Look in the air, on the water's surface and in the water. To help you to identify an insect, make a note of its colour, the shape and number of its wings, where you saw it and other details.

Remember that all adult insects have bodies with three parts, three pairs of legs, and usually a pair of antennae or feelers. Many have wings at some time in their lives.

Above the Water

Dragonflies fly in pairs when mating.

Swarms of **Mayflies** rise and fall over the water.

A **Damselfly** at rest holds its wings together.

A **Mayfly** has two or three long threads at the end of its body.

Look for these flying insects in spring and early summer, when they emerge from the pupa or nymph. Most stay close to the water, and they all breed there.

How Insects Stay on the Surface

Use blotting paper to place the needle on the water.

The paper will sink, but the needle will stay afloat.

A thin film on the surface of the water holds insects up. See how this works by floating a needle on water.

On the Surface

The **Pond Skater** slides rapidly over the surface. It can also jump.

The **Water Measurer** moves slowly. The hairs on its body stop it from getting wet.

Whirligig Beetles whirl and spin, without colliding, while looking for food.

Tiny **Springtails** can jump 30 cm using their hinged tails.

Notice the different ways that these insects move on the water surface. They feed mostly on dead insects that fall on the water.

Under the Water

Breathing tube

Its antenna breaks the surface film while it collects air.

The **Water Boatman** swims and takes in air at the surface, upside down.

It has strong legs for swimming.

Air bubble

Most insects breathe by taking in air through holes in their bodies. Many underwater insects carry a bubble of air on their bodies, which they collect at the surface and replace when it is used up.

The **Water Scorpion** takes in air at the surface through a breathing tube. It stores air under its wing cases.

The **Great Silver Beetle** carries a bubble of air trapped by the hairs on its underside.

How Insects Feed

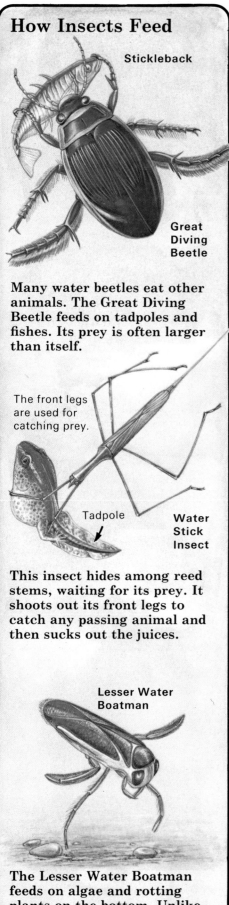

Stickleback

Great Diving Beetle

Many water beetles eat other animals. The Great Diving Beetle feeds on tadpoles and fishes. Its prey is often larger than itself.

The front legs are used for catching prey.

Tadpole

Water Stick Insect

This insect hides among reed stems, waiting for its prey. It shoots out its front legs to catch any passing animal and then sucks out the juices.

Lesser Water Boatman

The Lesser Water Boatman feeds on algae and rotting plants on the bottom. Unlike the Water Boatman, it swims right side up.

Making an Insect Aquarium

This picture shows the things you will need to make an aquarium. You can buy some of them at pet shops. Keep the aquarium near a window, but not in direct sunlight. If you use tap water, add some pond water and leave it for a few days before adding the animals.

Nymphs and Larvae

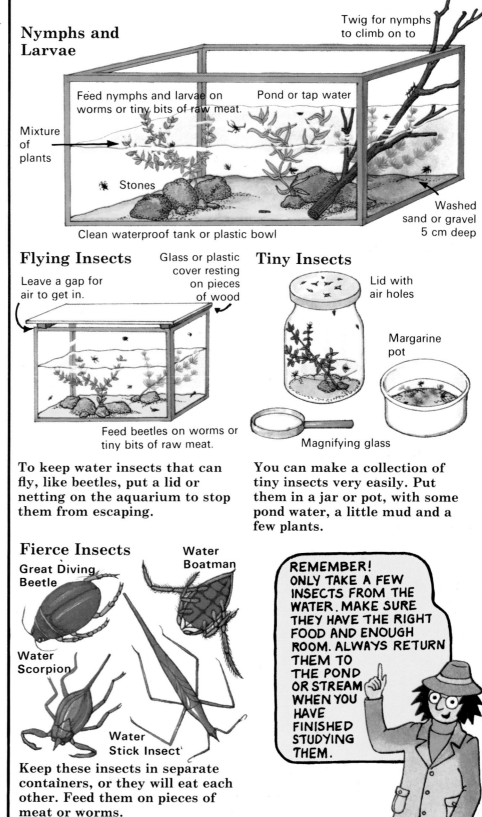

Twig for nymphs to climb on to

Feed nymphs and larvae on worms or tiny bits of raw meat.

Pond or tap water

Mixture of plants

Stones

Washed sand or gravel 5 cm deep

Clean waterproof tank or plastic bowl

Flying Insects

Leave a gap for air to get in.

Glass or plastic cover resting on pieces of wood

Feed beetles on worms or tiny bits of raw meat.

To keep water insects that can fly, like beetles, put a lid or netting on the aquarium to stop them from escaping.

Tiny Insects

Lid with air holes

Margarine pot

Magnifying glass

You can make a collection of tiny insects very easily. Put them in a jar or pot, with some pond water, a little mud and a few plants.

Fierce Insects

Great Diving Beetle

Water Boatman

Water Scorpion

Water Stick Insect

Keep these insects in separate containers, or they will eat each other. Feed them on pieces of meat or worms.

REMEMBER! ONLY TAKE A FEW INSECTS FROM THE WATER. MAKE SURE THEY HAVE THE RIGHT FOOD AND ENOUGH ROOM. ALWAYS RETURN THEM TO THE POND OR STREAM WHEN YOU HAVE FINISHED STUDYING THEM.

Mammals

Most mammals that live near fresh water are very shy and are not often seen. Some are nocturnal, which means that they are only active at night. Often all you will hear is a "plop" as the animal leaps into the water to get away. Mammals can hear well and have a good sense of smell. So if you go animal tracking, approach the water quietly, facing the wind. You may find animal tracks or feeding signs. Try to identify them, so that you know which animal you are looking for!

Spot the Difference

Water Vole — Tiny ears — Short, furry tail

Brown Rat — Large ears — Blunt snout — Pointed snout — Long, naked tail

The Water Vole is often confused with the Brown Rat. They look rather alike and both are often seen swimming. Look at the differences carefully, so that you can tell them apart if you spot them. The Water Vole often swims under the water, but the Brown Rat keeps more to the surface of the water.

The **Harvest Mouse**, driven out of the cornfields by farm machinery, now often nests in reed beds. It is an expert climber and can hang by its tail. It comes out in the day.

This bat often flies over water in the daytime, hunting for insects. It can swim well too.

Daubenton's Bat

The **Brown Rat** prefers rivers and canals. Look for it at any time of day. It eats almost anything.

The **Water Shrew** sometimes leaps out of the water to catch insects. It also eats fishes and frogs. You may see it walking on the bottom of streams, looking for food.

Look on banks of large ponds and slow rivers for the Water Vole. You may see it dive into the water. After a swim, it grooms its fur.

Look for plant stems which have been bitten off. This could be the feeding spot of a Water Vole.

Holes in the bank, either above or below water, could be the entrance to a **Shrew's** or **Vole's** burrow.

Rare Mammals

Muskrat

Beaver

European Mink

The Muskrat is a large vole that lives in parts of Europe, but not in Britain. It swims fast and keeps near the surface of shallow, overgrown water.

A few Beavers survive in Europe, mostly in remote northern areas. They build their homes, called lodges, with branches or logs that they cut from trees.

Some Minks are wild, while others have escaped from fur farms. You might see one in a reed bed or by a river. They hunt and swim at night. They are very fierce.

The Otter

When it dives for fish, it shuts its ears and nostrils.

Waterproof fur

Spraints

Its thick tail acts as a rudder.

Webbed toes for swimming

The Otter is a shy, nocturnal animal. It lives in lonely places, and is well adapted for life in the water. It eats fishes, frogs and shellfish. Otter cubs are born in a holt, a tunnel in the bank or among tree roots. Even the adults are playful and make slides down the river bank in the snow or mud. You might see one of these slides, or find Otter droppings, called spraints, on a rock or clump of grass. Otters often leave behind remains of fish they have eaten.

Tracks

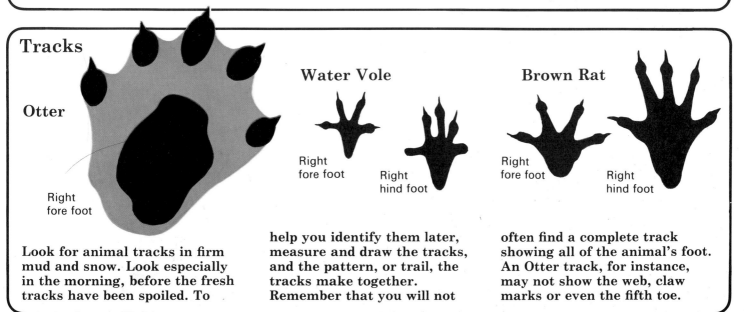

Otter

Right fore foot

Water Vole

Right fore foot

Right hind foot

Brown Rat

Right fore foot

Right hind foot

Look for animal tracks in firm mud and snow. Look especially in the morning, before the fresh tracks have been spoiled. To help you identify them later, measure and draw the tracks, and the pattern, or trail, the tracks make together. Remember that you will not often find a complete track showing all of the animal's foot. An Otter track, for instance, may not show the web, claw marks or even the fifth toe.

Fishes

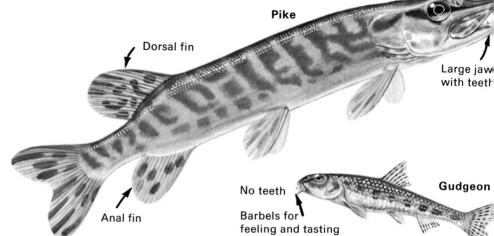

Pike

Dorsal fin

Large jaw with teeth

Anal fin

No teeth

Barbels for feeling and tasting

Gudgeon

There are nearly 40 kinds of freshwater fishes in Britain.

Notice which kinds prefer still or moving water, and make a check-list to help you to identify the fish: what colour and shape is it? Does it have whiskers, or barbels, near its mouth? Is it near the surface or on the bottom? How fast does it swim?

Most freshwater fishes spawn, or lay their eggs, in shallow water. Look for eggs among water plants and on the stones and sand of the bottom. Small fishes are called fry.

The fierce Pike, which grows up to 1m long, hunts frogs, young birds, fishes, and even other Pike. It lurks in reeds, waiting for its prey, and then attacks with its sharp teeth.

The Gudgeon is a bottom-feeder. It sucks insect larvae, worms and shellfish into its mouth. Its mouth is toothless, but it has teeth in its throat which break up the food it swallows.

In a Pond

Most pond fishes are rounder and fatter than the slim, streamlined fishes of running water. They swim more slowly too.

Perch egg bands

The **Carp** basks near the surface of warm, weedy ponds. It eats plants and sucks up mud to sift out worms and insects.

The **Perch** likes clean, shaded water. Look under bridges and overhanging trees. It eats small fishes.

Minnows

Ponds can become overcrowded with **Rudd**. The fish stay very small because there is not enough food for them.

The **Tench** lives among water plants and often lies buried in mud on the bottom of small ponds. It eats insects and snails.

1 Building a Nest

2

3

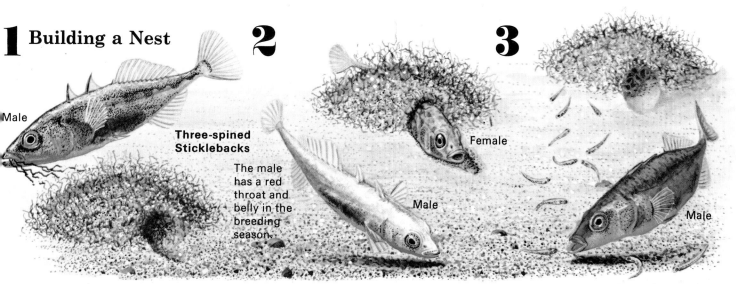

Male

Three-spined Sticklebacks

The male has a red throat and belly in the breeding season.

Female

Male

Male

Look for this Stickleback in ponds and ditches. In May, a male builds a nest where the female will lay her eggs. He glues bits of plants together with sticky threads from

his body. The male "dances" to attract a female to the nest. The female leaves after laying the eggs. The male then fans the eggs with his fins to keep fresh water

flowing over them. When the eggs hatch, the male guards the fry. He chases away enemies and catches stray fry in his mouth to bring them back to the nest.

In a Stream

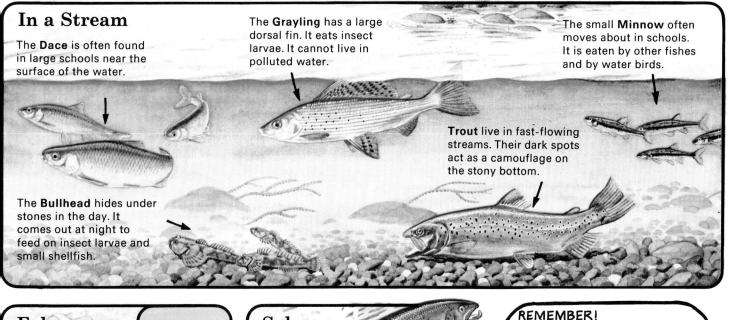

The **Dace** is often found in large schools near the surface of the water.

The **Grayling** has a large dorsal fin. It eats insect larvae. It cannot live in polluted water.

The small **Minnow** often moves about in schools. It is eaten by other fishes and by water birds.

Trout live in fast-flowing streams. Their dark spots act as a camouflage on the stony bottom.

The **Bullhead** hides under stones in the day. It comes out at night to feed on insect larvae and small shellfish.

Eels

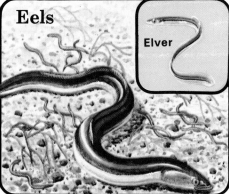

Elver

Eels live in fresh water until they are about ten years old. Then they move down rivers to the sea to breed and die. The young eels, called elvers, travel back to fresh water.

Salmon

Salmon spend some of their lives in the sea, but return to fresh water to breed. Most Salmon even reach the river where they were born. The female lays up to 15,000 eggs on the river bottom.

REMEMBER!
IF YOU WANT TO SEE FISHES, APPROACH THE WATER SLOWLY AND QUIETLY. KEEP YOUR SHADOW OFF THE WATER. TRY FEEDING FISHES WITH BREAD OR MAGGOTS.

Frogs, Toads and Newts

Frogs, toads and newts are born in water, but spend most of their adult life on land. These animals are called amphibians. The young tadpoles develop from eggs, called spawn, laid in the water. They breathe by taking in oxygen from the water through their gills. As they grow, their gills and tails slowly disappear, and lungs and legs take their place (although newts keep their tails). Now the young amphibian leaves the water except when it returns to the pond to breed in spring.

Frogs

Common Frog

Long tongue joined to the front of the mouth

Dark patches around its ears and on its back legs

Smooth, moist skin

Long back legs for jumping

Webbed toes for swimming

The Common Frog lives in damp grass and undergrowth. Its basic colour can change to match its surroundings. This helps it to hide from snakes, hedgehogs, rats and other enemies. In winter, the frog hibernates in the mud bottom of a ditch or pond.

How Frogs Breed

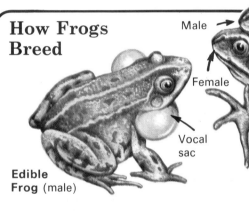

Male

Female

Common Frog

Vocal sac

Edible Frog (male)

Male's thumb pad

Frogspawn

Frogs breed in ponds. The males croak to attract females. The male Edible Frog blows up his vocal sacs, which makes the croak louder.

When mating, the male frog holds on to the female with his spiky thumb pads. The female lays a clump of spawn in the water.

A clump of frogspawn contains up to 4,000 eggs. The jelly around them swells with water and floats to the surface, where the sun warms the eggs.

How Frogspawn Develops

After four days, the tadpole can swim. Its mouth opens. It eats plants at first, then small animals as well.

The gills disappear and lungs form. The tadpole breathes at the surface.

Gland

Gills for breathing

The tadpole forms inside the egg and wriggles out after ten days.

The newly-hatched tadpole clings to a water plant with its sticky gland. Its mouth is still closed.

After eight weeks, the back legs form.

At 10 or 11 weeks, its front legs develop.

Toads

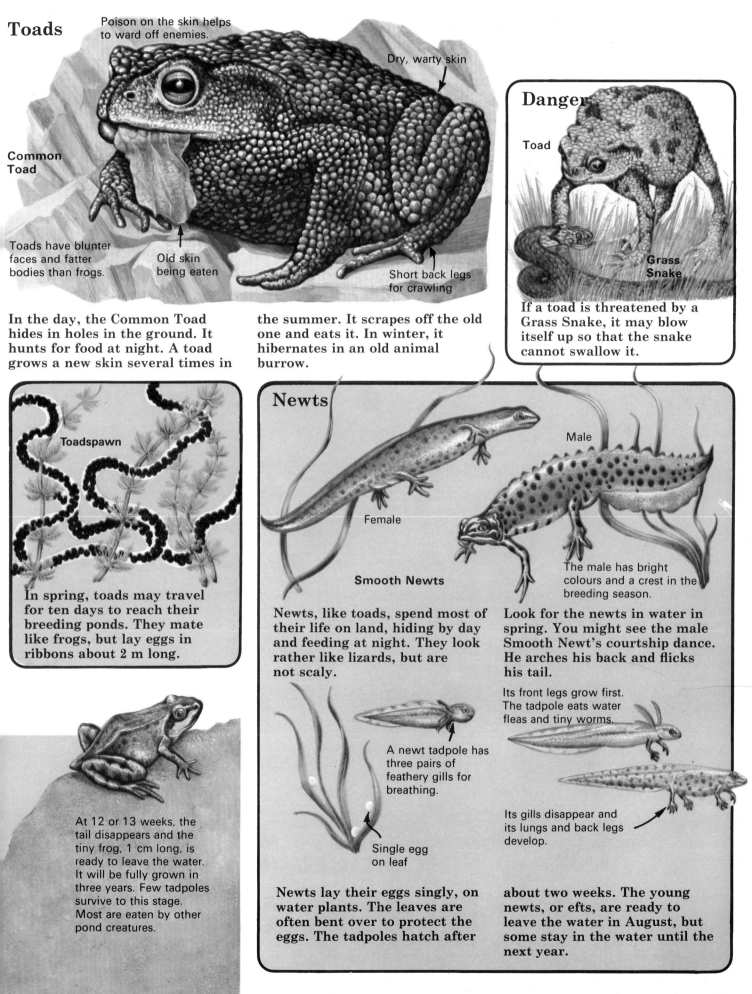

Poison on the skin helps to ward off enemies.

Dry, warty skin

Common Toad

Toads have blunter faces and fatter bodies than frogs.

Old skin being eaten

Short back legs for crawling

In the day, the Common Toad hides in holes in the ground. It hunts for food at night. A toad grows a new skin several times in the summer. It scrapes off the old one and eats it. In winter, it hibernates in an old animal burrow.

Danger

Toad

Grass Snake

If a toad is threatened by a Grass Snake, it may blow itself up so that the snake cannot swallow it.

Toadspawn

In spring, toads may travel for ten days to reach their breeding ponds. They mate like frogs, but lay eggs in ribbons about 2 m long.

At 12 or 13 weeks, the tail disappears and the tiny frog, 1 cm long, is ready to leave the water. It will be fully grown in three years. Few tadpoles survive to this stage. Most are eaten by other pond creatures.

Newts

Male

Female

Smooth Newts

The male has bright colours and a crest in the breeding season.

Newts, like toads, spend most of their life on land, hiding by day and feeding at night. They look rather like lizards, but are not scaly.

Look for the newts in water in spring. You might see the male Smooth Newt's courtship dance. He arches his back and flicks his tail.

A newt tadpole has three pairs of feathery gills for breathing.

Its front legs grow first. The tadpole eats water fleas and tiny worms.

Single egg on leaf

Its gills disappear and its lungs and back legs develop.

Newts lay their eggs singly, on water plants. The leaves are often bent over to protect the eggs. The tadpoles hatch after about two weeks. The young newts, or efts, are ready to leave the water in August, but some stay in the water until the next year.

Keeping Amphibians

Frogspawn

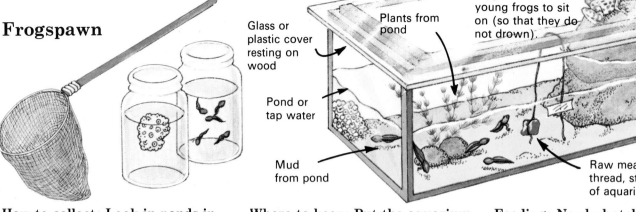

Glass or plastic cover resting on wood

Plants from pond

Large stone for young frogs to sit on (so that they do not drown).

Pond or tap water

Mud from pond

Raw meat tied on to thread, stuck to outside of aquarium with tape

How to collect: Look in ponds in March and April. Use a net to collect frogspawn. Put a little in a jar and return the rest to the water. If the eggs have already hatched, collect some tadpoles to study instead.

Where to keep: Put the aquarium in a light place, but out of direct sunlight. Change the water as soon as it smells bad. When the frogs have grown, return them to the edge of the pond where you found the spawn.

Feeding: Newly-hatched tadpoles will eat plants in the aquarium. After about a week, they will need raw meat too. Hang small pieces in the water, tied with thread, and replace them every two days.

Toads

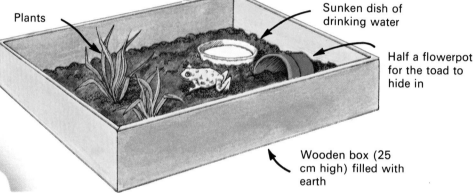

Plants

Sunken dish of drinking water

Half a flowerpot for the toad to hide in

Wooden box (25 cm high) filled with earth

How to collect: Visit ponds in the breeding season (March, April) at night. If you hear a male toad croaking, shine a torch at him. When the light hits his eyes, he will not move. Take the toad home in a wet plastic box with air holes.

Where to keep: Make a box like this. Put netting on top to keep the toad in. Put it in the shade, either in the garden or indoors. Handle it with wet hands. In the autumn, return it to the pond's edge, so that it can hibernate.

Feeding: Feed the toad twice a week with live earthworms, slugs and insects. Offer it small pieces of meat held in tweezers and moved about to look alive. Keep the dish filled with fresh water.

Newts

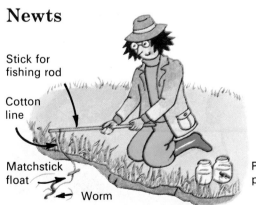

Stick for fishing rod

Cotton line

Matchstick float

Worm

Netting

Floating platform of wood or polystyrene for newts to sit on

Eggs

Pond plants

How to collect: In early spring, fish for newts or catch them in a net. When the newt bites the worm bait, pull the line in. Take it home in a jar with some pond water.

Where to keep: Keep newts in an aquarium in a light place. Take them back to the edge of the same pond in August, so that they can find a place to hibernate.

Feeding: If the newts mate and tadpoles hatch, feed them on Water Fleas from the pond. Feed adult newts on earthworms and small bits of raw meat dropped into the water.

Other Water Animals

Worms and Leeches

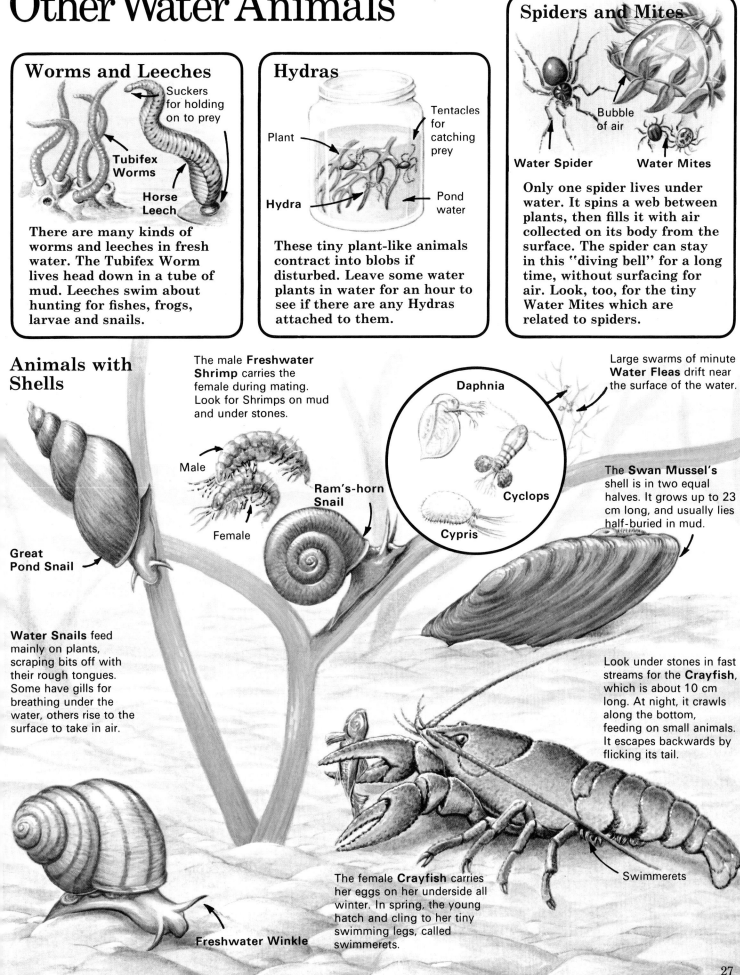

Suckers for holding on to prey

Tubifex Worms

Horse Leech

There are many kinds of worms and leeches in fresh water. The Tubifex Worm lives head down in a tube of mud. Leeches swim about hunting for fishes, frogs, larvae and snails.

Hydras

Plant

Tentacles for catching prey

Hydra

Pond water

These tiny plant-like animals contract into blobs if disturbed. Leave some water plants in water for an hour to see if there are any Hydras attached to them.

Spiders and Mites

Bubble of air

Water Spider   Water Mites

Only one spider lives under water. It spins a web between plants, then fills it with air collected on its body from the surface. The spider can stay in this "diving bell" for a long time, without surfacing for air. Look, too, for the tiny Water Mites which are related to spiders.

Animals with Shells

The male **Freshwater Shrimp** carries the female during mating. Look for Shrimps on mud and under stones.

Male

Female

Ram's-horn Snail

Daphnia

Cyclops

Cypris

Large swarms of minute **Water Fleas** drift near the surface of the water.

The **Swan Mussel's** shell is in two equal halves. It grows up to 23 cm long, and usually lies half-buried in mud.

Great Pond Snail

Water Snails feed mainly on plants, scraping bits off with their rough tongues. Some have gills for breathing under the water, others rise to the surface to take in air.

Look under stones in fast streams for the **Crayfish**, which is about 10 cm long. At night, it crawls along the bottom, feeding on small animals. It escapes backwards by flicking its tail.

The female **Crayfish** carries her eggs on her underside all winter. In spring, the young hatch and cling to her tiny swimming legs, called swimmerets.

Swimmerets

Freshwater Winkle

27

More Freshwater Life to Spot

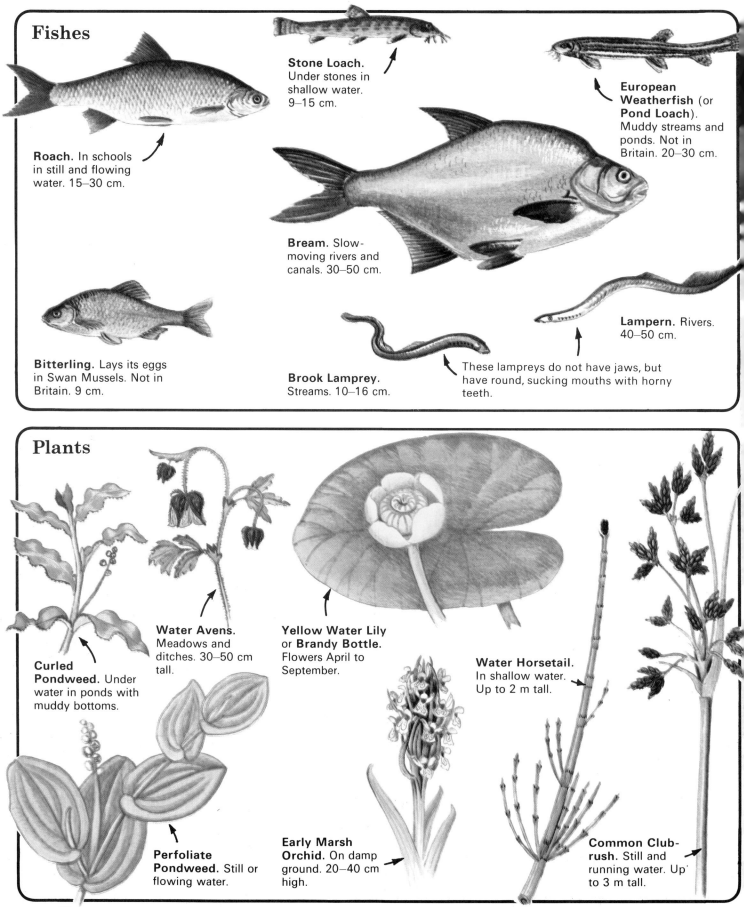

Fishes

Roach. In schools in still and flowing water. 15–30 cm.

Stone Loach. Under stones in shallow water. 9–15 cm.

European Weatherfish (or **Pond Loach**). Muddy streams and ponds. Not in Britain. 20–30 cm.

Bream. Slow-moving rivers and canals. 30–50 cm.

Bitterling. Lays its eggs in Swan Mussels. Not in Britain. 9 cm.

Brook Lamprey. Streams. 10–16 cm.

These lampreys do not have jaws, but have round, sucking mouths with horny teeth.

Lampern. Rivers. 40–50 cm.

Plants

Curled Pondweed. Under water in ponds with muddy bottoms.

Water Avens. Meadows and ditches. 30–50 cm tall.

Yellow Water Lily or **Brandy Bottle.** Flowers April to September.

Water Horsetail. In shallow water. Up to 2 m tall.

Perfoliate Pondweed. Still or flowing water.

Early Marsh Orchid. On damp ground. 20–40 cm high.

Common Club-rush. Still and running water. Up to 3 m tall.

If you cannot see the fish or plant you want to identify on this page, turn to the pages earlier in the book that deal with these things.

Toads

Common Toad. Hides under stones or tree roots in day. Often in gardens. Female to 12 cm. Male 6 cm.

Natterjack Toad. Sandy and stony places. Digs holes to shelter in. Rare. 6–8 cm.

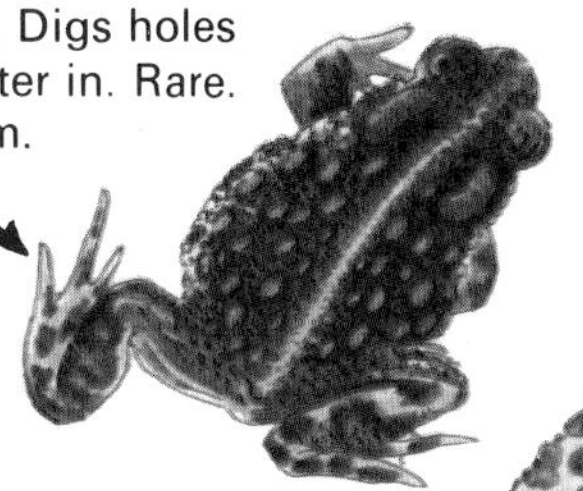

Green Toad. Green shade changes to match background. Not in Britain. 6–9 cm.

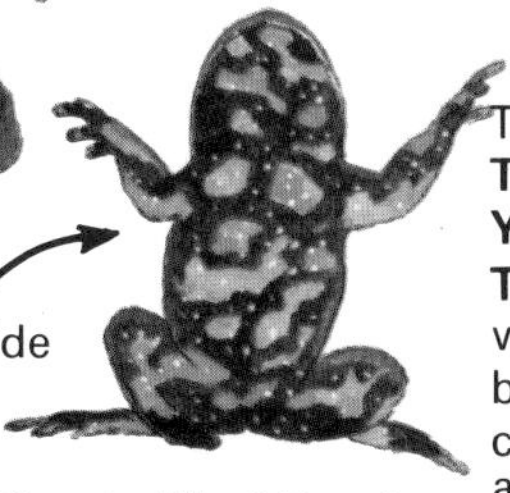

Yellow-bellied Toad

Underside

The **Fire-bellied Toad** and the **Yellow-bellied Toad** live in water. Show off bright warning colours when alarmed. Not in Britain. 4–5 cm.

Fire-bellied Toad

Spadefoot Toad. Burrows with spade-like growths on feet. Smells like garlic. Not in Britain. 6–8 cm.

Frogs

Common Frog. Damp shady places. Size and colour vary. 7–10 cm.

Painted Frog. Lives in water. France and Spain. 6–7 cm.

Parsley Frog. Near ponds in France, Italy and Spain. 4.5 cm.

European Tree Frog. In trees. Breeds in water. Not in Britain. 3–5 cm.

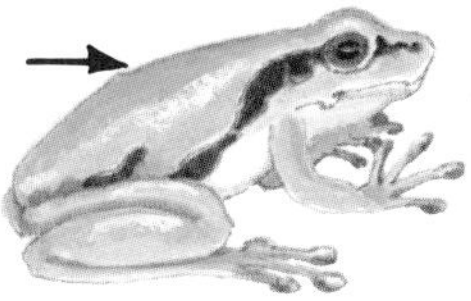

Edible Frog. Female larger than male. Near water. 7–10 cm.

Tortoise

European Pond Tortoise. Muddy ponds and marshes. Central and southern Europe. Up to 36 cm.

Newts

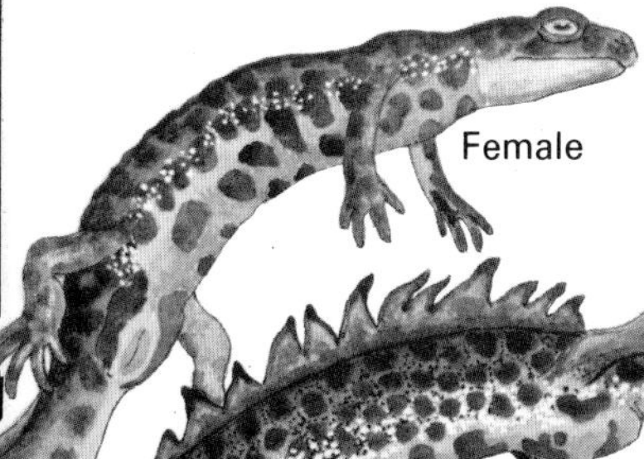

Male

Female

Palmate Newt. 8–9 cm.

Female

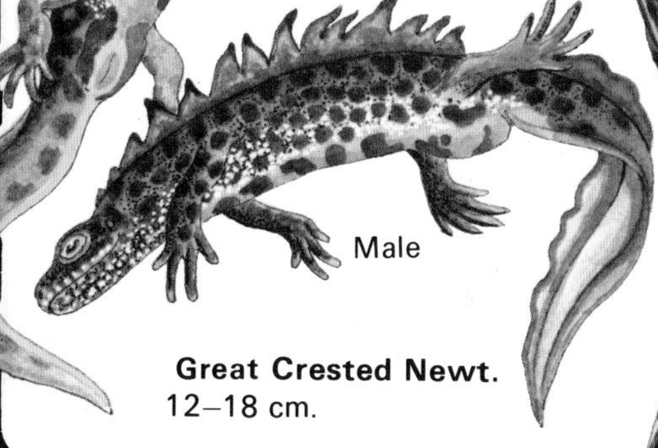

Male

Great Crested Newt. 12–18 cm.

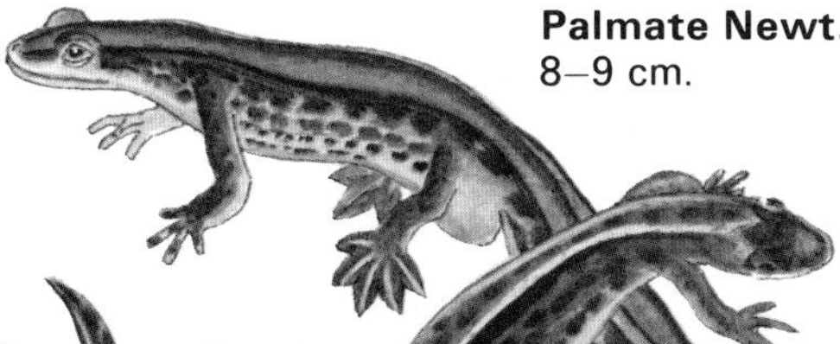

Male

Alpine Newt. Not in Britain. 7–12 cm.

Snakes

Viperine Snake. Often in water. Zigzag markings like Adder, but harmless. Southern Europe. 1 m.

Tesselated Snake. Very good swimmer. Central and southern Europe. 1.5 m.

All these frogs, toads and newts return to water to breed.

Water Insects and their Young

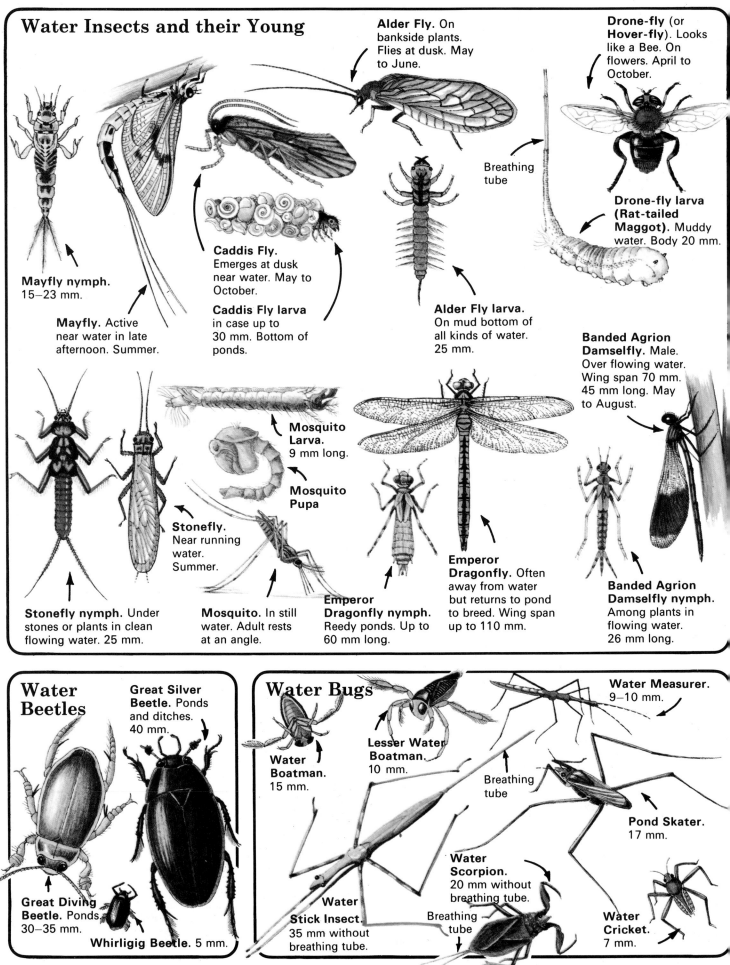

Alder Fly. On bankside plants. Flies at dusk. May to June.

Drone-fly (or Hover-fly). Looks like a Bee. On flowers. April to October.

Breathing tube

Drone-fly larva (Rat-tailed Maggot). Muddy water. Body 20 mm.

Mayfly nymph. 15–23 mm.

Mayfly. Active near water in late afternoon. Summer.

Caddis Fly. Emerges at dusk near water. May to October.

Caddis Fly larva in case up to 30 mm. Bottom of ponds.

Alder Fly larva. On mud bottom of all kinds of water. 25 mm.

Banded Agrion Damselfly. Male. Over flowing water. Wing span 70 mm. 45 mm long. May to August.

Mosquito Larva. 9 mm long.

Mosquito Pupa

Stonefly. Near running water. Summer.

Stonefly nymph. Under stones or plants in clean flowing water. 25 mm.

Mosquito. In still water. Adult rests at an angle.

Emperor Dragonfly nymph. Reedy ponds. Up to 60 mm long.

Emperor Dragonfly. Often away from water but returns to pond to breed. Wing span up to 110 mm.

Banded Agrion Damselfly nymph. Among plants in flowing water. 26 mm long.

Water Beetles

Great Silver Beetle. Ponds and ditches. 40 mm.

Great Diving Beetle. Ponds. 30–35 mm.

Whirligig Beetle. 5 mm.

Water Bugs

Water Boatman. 15 mm.

Lesser Water Boatman. 10 mm.

Water Measurer. 9–10 mm.

Breathing tube

Pond Skater. 17 mm.

Water Stick Insect. 35 mm without breathing tube.

Water Scorpion. 20 mm without breathing tube.

Breathing tube

Water Cricket. 7 mm.

If you cannot see the insect you want to identify on this page, turn to the pages earlier in the book on insects, where you may be able to see a picture of it.

Birds

Measurements are from beak to tip of tail.

Grey Heron. Nests in trees. Feeds in shallow water and marshes. 90 cm.

Osprey. Dives to catch fish in claws. Rare. A few breed in Scotland. 51–58 cm.

Mallard. Most common duck. Often in parks. 58 cm.

Male

Female

Chick

Great Crested Grebe. In lakes and reservoirs. Winters also on coast. 48 cm.

Winter

Summer

Female

Male

Teal. Europe's smallest duck. 35 cm.

Coot. Lives in flocks outside breeding season. Notice white mark on head. 38 cm.

Chick

Snipe. Hides among plants near water, where it feeds. Long bill for probing in mud. 27 cm.

Chick

Moorhen. Common in parks. Notice white flash under tail. 33 cm.

Water Rail. Hides in reed beds. 28 cm.

Summer

Winter

Black-headed Gull. Loses dark cap in winter. 35–38 cm.

Spotted Crake. White spotted body. Feeds at water edge at dusk. Very secretive. 23 cm.

Swallow. Summer visitor. Catches insects on the wing. 19 cm.

Yellow Wagtail. Lives in Britain. **Blue-headed Wagtail** in Central Europe. Other varieties in Europe (see below). 16.5 cm.

Yellow Wagtail

Pied Wagtail

Female

Blue-headed Wagtail

Scandinavia

White Wagtail. Lives in Europe. **Pied Wagtail** in Britain. 18 cm.

White Wagtail

Male

Grey Wagtail. Lives near fast-flowing streams. 18 cm.

Italy   Spain and France

Reed Bunting. By rivers and in marshy places. 15 cm.

If you cannot see the bird you want to identify on this page, turn to the pages earlier in the book on birds, and you may be able to see a picture of it.

Index

Books to Read

The Pond Book. John Dyson (Puffin Books)
The Ecology of Water Life. Alfred Leutscher (Franklin Watts)
Freshwater Animals in Clue Book series. Gwen Allen & Joan Denslow (Oxford)
Pond and Stream Life. John Clegg (Blandford)
The *Observer's Book of Pond Life.* John Clegg (Warne)
Your Book of Freshwater Life. John Clegg (Faber and Faber)
Pond and Marsh. James Whinray (A & C Black)
The Birds of Britain and Europe. Heinzel, Fitter and Parslow (Collins)
Reptiles and Amphibians. Hans Hvass (Blandford)

Clubs and Societies

The Council for Environmental Conservation (address: Zoological Gardens, Regent's Park, London NW1) will supply the addresses of your local **Natural History Societies.** (Send a stamped self-addressed envelope for the list.) Many of these have specialist sections and almost all have field meetings. **The Royal Society for Nature Conservation** (address: 22 The Green, Nettleham, Lincoln) will give you the address of your local **County Naturalist Trust,** which may have a junior branch. Many of the Trusts have meetings and lectures and offer opportunities for work on nature reserves.
The Mammal Society. For information about Youth Membership write to: Ms Lenton, 5 St Stephens Court, Bath, Avon.

The Amateur Entomologists' Society has younger members as well as adults. Write to: 355 Hounslow Road, Hanworth, Feltham, Middlesex.
The **Young Ornithologists' Club** (address: The Lodge, Sandy, Bedfordshire, SG19 SD1) is the junior section of **The Royal Society for the Protection of Birds** and helps young people to study bird life.
Other useful addresses:
Freshwater Biological Association, The Ferry House, Ambleside, Westmoreland.
Natural History Museum, South Kensington, London SW7.